The Holy Spirit Unleashed in You

Kay Arthur

HARVEST HOUSE PUBLISHERS
Eugene, Oregon 97402

Books in the International Inductive Study Series

Teach Me Your Ways: Genesis, Exodus, Leviticus, Numbers, Deuteronomy
The Call to Follow Jesus: Luke
Free from Bondage God's Way: Galatians, Ephesians
The Holy Spirit Unleashed in You: Acts

Cover illustration and interior art by Micha'el Washer

The International Inductive Study Series
THE HOLY SPIRIT UNLEASHED IN YOU

Copyright © 1994 Precept Ministries
Published by Harvest House Publishers
Eugene, Oregon 97402

Library of Congress Cataloging-in-Publication Data

Arthur, Kay, 1933–
    The Holy Spirit unleashed in you : Acts / Kay Arthur.
        p.   cm. — (International inductive study series)
    ISBN 1-56507-245-6
    1. Bible. N.T. Acts—Study and teaching. 2. Bible. N.T. Acts—Criticism, interpretation, etc. I. Title. II. Series: Arthur, Kay, 1933- International inductive study series.
BS2626.A78   1994
226.6'007—dc20   94-25522
                                                                      CIP

Printed in the United States of America.

95 96 97 98 99 00 — 10 9 8 7 6 5 4 3

CONTENTS

How to Get Started...

Reading directions is sometimes difficult and hardly ever enjoyable! Most often you just want to get started. Only if all else fails will you read the instructions. I understand, but please don't approach this study that way. These brief instructions are a vital part of getting started on the right foot! These few pages will help you immensely.

FIRST

As you study Acts, you will need four things in addition to this book:

1. A Bible that you are willing to mark in. The marking is essential. An ideal Bible for this purpose is *The International Inductive Study Bible (IISB)*. The *IISB* is in a single-column text format with larger, easy-to-read type, which is ideal for marking. The margins of the text are wide and blank for note-taking.

The *IISB* also has instructions for studying each book of the Bible, but it does not contain any commentary on the text, nor is it compiled from any theological stance. Its purpose is to teach you how to discern truth for yourself through the inductive method of study. (The various charts and maps that you will find in this study guide are taken from the *IISB*.)

Whatever Bible you use, just know you will need to mark in it, which brings me to the second item you will need...

2. A fine-point, four-color ballpoint pen or various colored fine-point pens that you can use to write in your Bible. Office supply stores should have these.

3. Colored pencils or an eight-color leaded Pentel pencil.

4. A composition book or a notebook for working on your assignments or recording your insights.

SECOND

1. As you study Acts, you will be given specific instructions for each day's study. These should take you between 20 and 30 minutes a day, but if you desire to spend more time than this, you will increase your intimacy with the Word of God and the God of the Word.

If you are doing this study within the framework of a class and you find the lessons too heavy, then simply do what you can. To do a little is better than to do nothing. Don't be an "all or nothing" person when it comes to Bible study.

Remember, any time you get into the Word of God, you enter into more intensive warfare with the enemy. Why? Every piece of the Christian's armor is related to the Word of God. And our one and only offensive weapon is the sword of the Spirit, which is the Word of God. The enemy wants you to have a dull sword. Don't cooperate! You don't have to!

2. As you read each chapter, train yourself to ask the "5 W's and an H": who, what, when, where, why, and how. Asking questions like these helps you see exactly what the Word of God is saying. When you interrogate the text with the 5 W's and an H, you ask questions like these:

a. **What** is the chapter about?

b. **Who** are the main characters?

c. **When** does this event or teaching take place?

d. **Where** does this happen?

    e. **Why** is this being done or said?

    f. **How** did it happen?

    3. The "when" of events or teachings is very important and should be marked in an easily recognizable way in your Bible. I do this by putting a clock (like the one shown here) in the margin of my Bible beside the verse where the time phrase occurs. You may want to underline or color the references to time in one specific color.

    4. You will be given certain key words to mark throughout the book of Acts. This is the purpose of the colored pencils and the colored pen. If you will develop the habit of marking your Bible in this way, you will find it will make a significant difference in the effectiveness of your study and in how much you remember.

    A **key word** is an important word that is used by the author repeatedly in order to convey his message to his reader. Certain key words will show up throughout the book; others will be concentrated in specific chapters or segments of the book. When you mark a key word, you should also mark its synonyms (words that mean the same thing in the context) and any relative pronouns (*he, his, she, her, it, we, they, us, our, their, them*) in the same way you have marked the key word. I will give you suggestions for ways to mark key words in your daily assignments.

    Marking words for easy identification can be done by colors or symbols or a combination of colors and symbols. However, colors are easier to distinguish than symbols. If I use symbols, I keep them very simple. For example, I color *repent* yellow but put a red diagram like this over it repent. The symbol conveys the meaning of the word. When marking key words, mark them in a way that is easy for you to remember.

    When I mark the members of the Godhead (which I do not always mark), I color each word yellow. But I also use a purple

pen and mark the Father with a triangle like this $\triangle$, symboliz-
ing the Trinity. I mark the Son this way _⟍, and the Holy
Spirit this way ⌢⌣.

You should devise a color-coding system for marking key
words throughout your Bible so that when you look at the
pages of your Bible, you will see instantly where a key word is
used.

When you start marking key words, it is easy to forget how
you are marking them. I recommend cutting a three-by-five
card in half lengthwise and writing the key words on that.
Color-code the words and then use the card as a bookmark.
You may want to make one bookmark for words you are marking throughout your Bible and a different one for any specific
book of the Bible you are studying.

5. Because locations are important in a historical or bio-
graphical book of the Bible (and Acts is a historical book), you
will also find it helpful to mark locations in a distinguishable
way. I simply underline every reference to location in green
(grass and trees are green!) using my four-color ballpoint pen.
Maps have been included in this study so you can look up the
locations in order to put yourself into context geographically.

6. A chart called ACTS AT A GLANCE is located at the
end of your study guide. As you complete your study of each
chapter, record the main theme of that chapter under the
appropriate chapter number. The main theme of a chapter is
what the chapter deals with the most. It may be an event or a
particular subject or teaching. Usually in a historical or bio-
graphical book, the chapter themes center on events.

If you will fill out the ACTS AT A GLANCE chart as you
progress through the study, you will have a complete synopsis
of the book when you are finished. If you have an *International
Inductive Study Bible*, you will find the same chart in your Bible
(page 1820). If you will record your chapter themes there,
you'll always have them for a ready reference.

7. Always begin your study with prayer. As you do your part to handle the Word of God accurately, you must remember that the Bible is a divinely inspired book. The words that you are reading are truth, given to you by God so you can know Him and His ways more intimately. These truths are divinely revealed.

> For to us God revealed them through the Spirit; for the Spirit searches all things, even the depths of God. For who among men knows the thoughts of a man except the spirit of the man, which is in him? Even so the thoughts of God no one knows except the Spirit of God (1 Corinthians 2:10,11).

Therefore ask God to reveal His truth to you as He leads and guides you into all truth. He will, if you will ask.

8. Each day when you finish your lesson, meditate on what you saw. Ask your heavenly Father how you should live in light of the truths you have just studied. At times, depending on how God has spoken to you through His Word, you might even want to record these "Lessons for Life" in the margin of your Bible next to the text you have studied. Simply put "LFL" in the margin of your Bible, and then, as briefly as possible, record the lesson for life that you want to remember.

THIRD

This study is set up so that you have an assignment for every day of the week—so that you are in the Word daily. If you work through your study in this way, you will find it more profitable than doing a week's study in one sitting. Pacing yourself this way allows time for thinking through what you learn on a daily basis!

The seventh day of each week has different features than the other six days. These features are designed to aid group discussion; however, they are also profitable if you are studying this book individually.

The "seventh" day is whatever day in the week you choose to finish your week's study. On this day, you will find a verse or two for you to memorize and STORE IN YOUR HEART. Then there is a passage to READ AND DISCUSS. This will help you focus on a major truth or major truths covered in your study that week.

To assist those using the material in a Sunday school class or a group Bible study, there are OPTIONAL QUESTIONS FOR DISCUSSION. Even if you are not doing this study with anyone else, it would be good for you to answer these questions. *

If you are in a group, be sure every member of the class, including the teacher, supports his or her answers and insights from the Bible text itself. Then you will be handling the Word of God accurately. As you learn to see what the text says, the Bible explains itself.

Always examine your insights by carefully observing the text to see what it *says*. Then, before you decide what the passage of Scripture *means*, make sure that you interpret it in the light of its context. Scripture will never contradict Scripture. If it ever seems to contradict the rest of the Word of God, you can be certain that something is being taken out of context. If you come to a passage that is difficult to understand, reserve your interpretations for a time when you can study the passage in greater depth.

---

*Audio- and videotapes are being produced on each of these courses. Some of them are being aired on the radio or on television. If you would like information on whether these programs are aired in your area, contact Precept Ministries' Information Department, P.O. Box 182218, Chattanooga, Tennessee 37422, 615/892-6814.

The purpose of A THOUGHT FOR THE WEEK is to share with you what I consider to be an important element in your week of study. I have included it for your evaluation and, hopefully, for your edification. This section will help you see how to walk in light of what you learned.

Books in *The International Inductive Study Series* are survey courses. If you want to do a more in-depth study of a particular book of the Bible, we suggest you do a Precept Upon Precept Bible study course on that book. You may obtain more information on these courses by filling out and mailing the response card in the back of this book.

ACTS

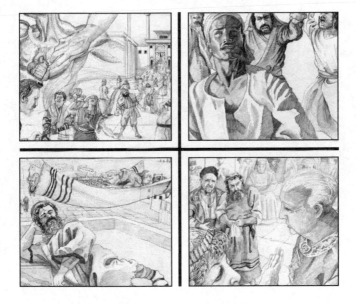

The Holy Spirit Unleashed in You...

How are you living, my friend? Is the Christian life a struggle for you? Do you feel defeated, powerless, and, therefore, impotent? If your life seems unproductive even though you are involved in all sorts of "Christian" activities, maybe you are not aware of what it means to "walk by the Spirit." Or maybe, like me and many others who sat in church most of their lives, you have a religion but not a relationship with the living God.

When Paul wrote his letter to the Galatians, he said, "If we live by the Spirit, let us also walk by the Spirit" (5:25). Your problem could be that you are a church member but not a member of the body of Christ, so you therefore aren't living by the Spirit. Or the problem could be that although you are truly a child of God, you are not filled with the Holy Spirit—you are not walking by the Spirit. If taken to heart, our study of the book of Acts, *The Holy Spirit Unleashed in You*, should solve your problem!

I stand on tiptoe in anticipation, eager to catch a glimpse of what our Father is going to do in your life and in the kingdom as you learn the lessons of Acts and are unleashed by the Spirit!

In the Gospels, Jesus Christ is front and center as we focus on His life, death, burial, and resurrection. In the book of Acts, the Holy Spirit comes front and center, because He is the fulfillment of Jesus' promise to send the Spirit after He ascended to the Father. As you work through Acts, you will want to learn all you can about the Spirit of God and about what your relationship to Him is to be. As you focus on your relationship with the Holy Spirit, you will discover many other invaluable truths that relate to living and walking by the Spirit.

Witnessing: God's Plan—
The Holy Spirit: God's Provision

DAY ONE

Read Acts 1. Discerning the author's purpose for writing and seeing how he structures his material to achieve his purpose is always valuable in studying any book of the Bible. As you read Acts 1, note who the author is, to whom the book is written, and why it is written. It is not the norm to find all of this information in one chapter, especially the first chapter, but you can find all of it in Acts 1! The purpose of the book of Acts is not spelled out in so many words, but you may still be able to find the reason. If you do not see the purpose today, I'll help you see it tomorrow, so give it a try. Write your insights in your notebook.

DAY TWO

Read Acts 1:1-3 again and then read the Gospel of Luke 1:1-14. Note who writes Luke, to whom it is written, and why. Again record your insights in your notebook.

The book of Acts is a continuation of what Jesus began in Luke! Acts is "Part 2" of Luke's story, but in Acts the focus shifts from the life of Jesus because He ascends to the Father. However, He does not go without leaving the disciples a promise in Acts 1.

Read Acts 1 again today. As you read, mark every reference to the *Holy Spirit*.[1] As you mark the words, notice what actions or activities are connected with the Spirit. Include these in your marking. For example, in Acts 1:5 mark the whole phrase *baptized with the Holy Spirit* and in 1:8 mark *power when the Holy Spirit has come upon you* just like you mark *Holy Spirit*.

Whenever I mark a reference to the Holy Spirit in my Bible, I always mark it the same way in the same colors. I underline the reference, color it yellow, and then diagram it this way: ⌒⌒⌒. You should put *Holy Spirit* on your bookmark because you will want to mark references to Him throughout the book of Acts. As you work through Acts, you will see the Holy Spirit referred to in different ways. You may want to add these to your bookmark as you come to them so that you will always be alert to them if they occur again. (I told you how and why to make your bookmark in the section called "How to Get Started." You did read it, didn't you?)

Now, according to Acts 1 what were the disciples promised? Write it in your notebook.

DAY THREE

Read Acts 1:1-5 again. By the way, if you will read Scripture aloud repeatedly, you will find yourself memorizing it.

Jesus promises believers they will be baptized with the Holy Spirit. To see where this promise is recorded, read the following passages: Matthew 3:11; Mark 1:8; Luke 3:16; and John 1:33. You may want to record these cross-references in the margin of your Bible next to Acts 1:4,5.

Cross-references are notes in the margin of your Bible that

---

[1]KJV: *Holy Ghost*

identify the location of another verse or passage that says the
same thing as the verse or passage under study or that rein-
forces a truth in those verses. Since you may not always have
study notes with you, having cross-references written in your
Bible can be very helpful! To mark this cross-reference, write
Mark 1:8 in the margin next to Matthew 3:11. Then by Mark
1:8 write Luke 3:16, and by Luke 3:16, John 1:33. So if you can
remember Matthew 3:11, you can trace this truth through the
Gospels.

There is only one other New Testament reference to the
baptism of the Holy Spirit outside of Acts and the ones just
noted in the Gospels. It is 1 Corinthians 12:13. You may want
to record it as a cross-reference also.

By the way, look at Acts 1:4. When they were told "to wait
for what the Father had promised," what was it they were to
wait for? You may want to mark *what the Father had promised*[2]
the same way you marked *Holy Spirit* in the other verses.

DAY FOUR

Read Acts 1 again. This time mark the following words
(along with their synonyms and pronouns), each in their own
distinctive way. I will tell you how I mark mine because people
often ask me how I mark my Bible.

> a. *witness (witnesses)*—I color the inside yellow
> because that is my color for the Father, Son, and
> Holy Spirit, and I am to be their witness about
> Jesus Christ so people can come to the Father
> and be indwelt by the Spirit! Then I box it in

---

[2]NIV: *the gift my Father promised*
  KJV; NKJV: *the promise of the Father*

orange (because that is one of my colors in my Pentel pencil!).

b. *resurrection* (any phrase that refers to the resurrection)—As you will see, the resurrection is an important part of our witness. I color this brown (Jesus was dead, buried) and then box it in with yellow (He lives!).

c. *prayer (prayed, pray, supplication)*—Although *pray* is not used in chapter 1, add it to your bookmark. It is used later in the book.

Add these key words to your bookmark. Don't forget to mark every reference to the Holy Spirit all the way through your study of Acts. By the way, in Acts 1:4 a synonym for *Holy Spirit* will be *promised.*[3]

DAY FIVE

Yesterday you read Acts 1 and marked every reference to the resurrection. Did you mark the phrase *He also presented Himself alive*[4] in Acts 1:3? Remember, you were going to mark references to Jesus' resurrection the same way you marked the word *resurrection*. If you happened to miss the phrase, mark it now.

In Acts 1:22 you read that "one of these [one of the men the disciples were selecting to take Judas' place] should become a witness with us of His resurrection." You saw that it

---

[3]KJV; NKJV: *promise*
[4]NIV: *he showed himself . . . that he was alive*
  KJV: *he shewed himself alive*

was required that the man witnessed the resurrection. Why? Because the resurrection is a key element throughout the Gospels.

Read 1 Corinthians 15:1-11. Mark the word *gospel*. I draw a blue megaphone like this ⟨gospel⟩ and then color it red. As you read this passage, note what Paul delivered (preached to them) and you will see the essence of the gospel. As you read, also note the phrase "according to the Scriptures."

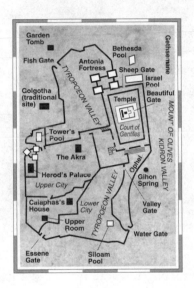

Record what you learn about the gospel in your notebook. You should set aside a couple of pages for this list so that you can go back and add insights to it as you work through Acts.

DAY SIX

Read Acts 1 again. Acts is a historical book that gives witnesses' accounts of Jesus' life, death, and resurrection.

Locations are important in Acts, so underline in green, or whatever color you prefer, every reference to a city or region (i.e., *Judea, Samaria*). There's a map of Jerusalem on page 21 you may want to consult in order to gain a perspective of the locations you mark. Also, the map below shows Jerusalem, Judea, and Samaria.

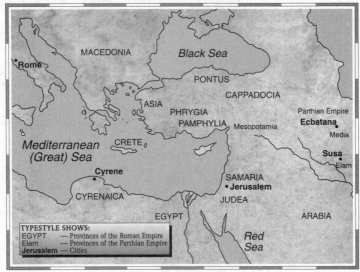

Jerusalem, Judea, and Samaria

Set aside several pages in your notebook for compiling a list on what you learn about the Holy Spirit as you work through Acts. Now, record your insights on the Holy Spirit from chapter 1.

For example, you would want to record the following:

Jesus gave orders by the Holy Spirit (1:2)

The Holy Spirit was promised by the Father (1:4)

Apostles would be baptized with the Holy Spirit (1:5)

As you see, the verse where the insight is found is listed beside it. When you review a completed list, it is often helpful to have the Scripture reference noted.

DAY SEVEN

💟Store in your heart: Acts 1:8.
Read and discuss: Acts 1:1-11.

OPTIONAL QUESTIONS FOR DISCUSSION

∾ When you made a list of what you learned about the Holy Spirit from Acts 1, what did you write down?

∾ The word for baptized in the Greek[5] is *baptizō* and it means "to dip, immerse, to submerge for religious purposes, overwhelm, saturate, baptize." It carries with it the idea of identification, of being united with someone or something. Compare Acts 1:5 with 1:8. When the apostles were baptized with the Holy Spirit, what would the Holy Spirit do through them?

∾ According to Acts 1:8, what would the apostles receive, and be, when the Holy Spirit came upon them (when they were baptized with the Holy Spirit)?

∾ Look at the places in Acts 1 where you marked *witnesses* and *witness*. What do you learn from observing the text in these verses?

---

[5]From time to time we will look at the definition of a word in the Greek. Since the New Testament was originally written in Koine Greek, sometimes it is helpful to go back to the Greek to see the original meaning of a word. There are many study tools to help you if you would like to do this type of digging. One excellent book that will help you understand how to do more in-depth study like this is *How to Study Your Bible* published by Harvest House Publishers.

∾ Where were the disciples to wait for the promise from the Father—the baptism of the Holy Spirit?

   a. Where were they to go once they received the baptism of the Holy Spirit?

   b. What were they to do? (This question may seem a little redundant after discussing what you learned about being witnesses, but it is good to reiterate these insights. Repetition is key to the learning process.)

   c. If you were to read the entire book of Acts before beginning this study, you would see that Acts is an account of how Acts 1:8 was fulfilled in those beginning days of the church. Thus, Acts can be divided into major portions as the account is given of how the gospel is taken to Jerusalem, Judea, Samaria, and to the uttermost parts of the earth. Acts continues today as we spread the gospel throughout the earth. As you study, watch where the gospel is taken, who takes it there, and when.

∾ What did you learn about the gospel from 1 Corinthians 15:1-11?

   a. If one is to preach the gospel, what points do you think are necessary to cover? Stick with what you see in the Scripture!

   b. What does the burial of Jesus confirm?

   c. What does the fact that He was seen by many confirm?

   d. Should one discuss sin when presenting the gospel? How do you know from this passage? Do you see this happening today as churches seek to reach the lost? What if the church tells you not to mention sin to lost people? What would you say?

   e. What part of witnessing is hardest for you? Do you witness very often? Why or why not?

∾ Spend time together in prayer. Let each person have an
opportunity to pray and to ask God to speak to them
through the study of Acts, to show them what it means to
live and to walk by the Spirit of God, to know His power,
and to be witnesses of Him.

THOUGHT FOR THE WEEK

Whenever God calls you to do something for Him, He
always supplies the means. You never have to do anything in
your own strength, wisdom, or power. You have the Holy
Spirit. He is your Helper.

How well Jesus Christ, the God-Man, demonstrated this as
He lived a life without sin. Man was to live in this way too, but
Adam and Eve chose to walk independently of God; to be like
God, knowing good and evil. The Gospel of John clearly states
that Jesus always and only did those things which pleased the
Father. The works that the Father did, the Son did also. The
words that the Father spoke were the words His Son spoke.
Jesus demonstrated how we, as mankind, are to live.

In Acts 1:2 you see that Jesus even gave orders to the
apostles by the Holy Spirit. May our Father show us over and
over again in this study of Acts what it means to be filled with
the Holy Spirit, to live in total dependence on God, to do
nothing apart from Him.

What Made
the Church Distinctive?
Are We Missing Something?

DAY ONE

Read Acts 2. Mark every reference to the *Holy Spirit* (*Spirit*)[6] in the same way you marked it last week. Remember to mark any action or activity of the Spirit in the same way you mark *Holy Spirit*. You will want to mark His action throughout the book. Also remember to mark the word *promise*[7] if it refers to the Holy Spirit, along with any pronouns such as *this*.[8]

Also add *believe (believes, believed)* to your bookmark. Mark these words throughout the book. You may want to begin a list of all that you learn by marking these words and add to it as you work through the book. It will be time-consuming but very helpful!

DAY TWO

Read Acts 2 again today. Mark the key words listed on your bookmark along with their synonyms and pronouns. Be sure not to miss *raised Him up again* and *raised up*[9] as references to

---

[6]KJV: *Holy Ghost*
[7]NIV: also uses *promised*
[8]NIV: *what*
[9]NIV: *raised him from the dead, raised*

the resurrection. In addition to the words already on your bookmark, add *in the name of Jesus Christ* and mark this phrase in a distinctive way.

DAY THREE

Read Acts 2:1-21. As you read, mark any references to time. Remember, I mark time references with a clock like this ⏰ , or I put the clock in the margin next to any verse which gives an indication of when something is happening or will happen.

Carefully observe the text. Note every reference to the Holy Spirit. Examine it in the light of the 5 W's and an H. Watch *to whom* the Holy Spirit is given, *when* the Spirit is given, *what* happens when the Spirit fills the people, *how* Peter explains what is happening, *who* the promise of the Holy Spirit is for, and *how* the gift of the Holy Spirit is received. Then, list all you learn about the Holy Spirit from this chapter in your notebook under the section on the Holy Spirit.

Do you see any relationship between Acts 2 and Acts 1? If you do, record your insights in your notebook.

DAY FOUR

Read Acts 2:14-21 and 2:32-42 and compare it with John 7:37-39; 14:16-18,25,26; 15:26,27; 16:7-15; and Romans 8:9,11,14-17. In each passage mark every reference to the *Holy Spirit (Spirit, Helper,* [10] *Spirit of truth, Spirit of God, Spirit of Christ).* Remember too to mark the pronouns. Then once again list everything you learn from these passages about the Holy Spirit in your notebook. As you do, note from what book, chapter, and verse you get your information.

When you finish, review the promise regarding the Holy Spirit that Jesus made in the Gospels (Matthew 3:11; Mark 1:8; Luke 3:16; and John 1:33). Note how these verses and promises complement and supplement your understanding of the promise in Acts 1, the day of Pentecost in Acts 2, and 1 Corinthians 12:13.

Today's work may take longer than your other days' assignments, but give it all the time you can. You'll find this study very profitable and enlightening.

Deal with the Scriptures with integrity. Never add to them or take away from them. Simply let God's Word explain what He's recorded in His Book. Remember, it is truth.

DAY FIVE

Read Acts 2:22-36 very carefully. Then list in your notebook the main points of Peter's message to the men of Israel.

DAY SIX

Read Acts 2:37-47. Note the people's response to Peter's message and what he tells them to do. As you observe these

---

[10]NIV: *Counselor*
   KJV: *Comforter*

final verses of Acts 2, examine them in the light of the 5 W's and an H.

Also make a list in your notebook of everything you learn in Acts 2:42-47 about the early believers. What do you think would happen if the church lived this way today?

Although the words *repent* and *repentance* are not used extensively throughout the book of Acts, they are key. So add these to your bookmark and be sure to mark them from this point on. (Remember I showed you how I mark the word *repent* in the "How to Get Started" section.) To repent is to have a change of mind. A genuine change of mind brings a change in your thinking, direction, or behavior.

Finally, my friend, at the end of this study book you will find a chart entitled ACTS AT A GLANCE. On this chart there is a place for you to record the theme of each chapter in Acts. The theme of a chapter is a summary of the main teaching or subject of that chapter. Sometimes there is more than one main theme; sometimes you will find two themes. For chapters 1 and 2, state as briefly as possible what those main themes are.

From now on as you complete your survey of each chapter of Acts, you will want to record the theme of that chapter. This is such a profitable exercise because when you finish you will have a synopsis of the content of the book.

You will also notice a place to record the date, author, and purpose. When you discover this information, record it in the appropriate places. Acts was probably written about A.D. 61.

DAY SEVEN

Store in your heart: Acts 2:38,39.
Read and discuss: Acts 2:12-21; Ephesians 2:11-22.

OPTIONAL QUESTIONS FOR DISCUSSION

ᦉ Exactly what happened on the day of Pentecost? Was there any relationship between this event and what you studied in Acts 1 last week? How do you know?

ᦉ How does Jesus' promise in Matthew 3:11; Mark 1:8; Luke 3:16; and John 1:33 relate to Acts 1? What is the correlation between the promise and what happened on the day of Pentecost?

ᦉ Was the promise of the baptism of the Holy Spirit only for the apostles? Read Acts 2:39 and 1 Corinthians 12:13. What do you learn from these verses?

    a. Now read Ephesians 1:13. What does this verse tell you about the believer and his relationship to the Holy Spirit?

    b. Read Ephesians 2:11-22. What do you learn from this passage about the body of Jesus Christ? Who is part of Jesus' body? What gives them access to the Father? What does verse 22 tell you about your relationship to the Holy Spirit?

ᦉ There is a chart on the feasts of Israel on pages 34 and 35. Look at this chart. What do you learn from it about the festival of Pentecost? On that day, the high priest would wave two loaves of bread taken from one lump of dough before the Lord. What do you think the two loaves of bread were a picture of? Read Ephesians 3:4-6. In Acts 10 we will study about the first Gentile converts to Christianity and how they also received the Holy Spirit.

ᦉ When Peter explained what happened on the day of Pentecost, he quoted from Joel 2:28-32, saying that in the last days God would pour forth His Spirit upon all mankind. Read Hebrews 1:2 and discuss what this verse says the last days are.

∾ According to all you have seen this week in the Word of God, how would you explain the baptism of the Holy Spirit? Look at your notes on the Holy Spirit that you collected from the Gospel of John.

∾ By the way, according to Acts 2:37-47, who added souls to the church? Was it done by compromising the message?

THOUGHT FOR THE WEEK

In the Old Testament days, the Holy Spirit came upon prophets, priests, and kings but He did not indwell them, sealing them for the day of their redemption. Rather, the Holy Spirit came and went. This is why David prayed, "Do not take Thy Holy Spirit from me" (Psalm 51:11). However, when Jesus came as the Lamb of God, He died for our sins and rose from the dead because of our justification. Then the promise of the indwelling of the Holy Spirit could be given to all who would repent and call upon the name of the Lord—both Jew and Gentile.

This promise was inaugurated on the day God ordained— the day of Pentecost—50 days after the resurrection of the Lord Jesus Christ on the feast of firstfruits. The sacrifice of Christ our Passover, the feast of unleavened bread, and the feast of firstfruits, along with the festival of Pentecost, were all pictures of our Redeemer and His awesome plan of the redemption of man.

When the Holy Spirit came, He then placed you in the body of Christ, giving you access to the Father. When you heard the message of the gospel and believed, you were sealed with the Holy Spirit until the day of your redemption.

When you are saved, you are baptized by the Spirit into the body of Christ. You have passed from death to life. You live by the Spirit. And it is His indwelling Spirit that bears witness with your spirit that you are a child of God.

Now, Beloved, the question is, "Where is the Spirit of God in relationship to you? Have you genuinely been born again by the Spirit of God" (John 3:1-10)? If not, won't you repent and have a change of mind about who Jesus Christ is? He is God, and He is the only Lord and Savior. Will you not call on Him to save you from your sins and to give you the gift of eternal life through Jesus Christ our Lord? If you will call, He will save you and give you the awesome gift of the Holy Spirit, who will place you in the body of Christ and indwell you as your resident Helper, Comforter, and Teacher. Then, Beloved, you will know how to live . . . and you'll be able to live forever and ever and ever.

THE FEASTS OF ISRAEL

Slaves in Egypt	1st Month (Nisan) Festival of Passover				3rd Month (Sivan) Festival of Pentecost
	Passover	Unleavened Bread	Firstfruits		Pentecost or Feast of Weeks
	Kill lamb & put blood on doorpost Exodus 12:6, 7	*Purging of all leaven* (symbol of sin)	*Wave offering of sheaf* (promise of harvest to come)		*Wave offering of two loaves of leavened bread*
	1st month 14th day Leviticus 23:5	1st month, 15th day for 7 days Leviticus 23:6-8	Day after Sabbath Leviticus 23:9-14		50 days after Firstfruits Leviticus 23:15-21
Whosoever commits sin is the slave to sin	Christ our Passover has been sacrificed	Clean out old leaven... just as you are in fact unleavened	Christ has been raised...the firstfruits	Going away so Comforter can come	Promise of the Spirit, mystery of church: Jews-Gentiles in one body
				Mount of Olives	
John 8:34	1 Corinthians 5:7	1 Corinthians 5:7, 8	1 Corinthians 15:20-23	John 16:7 Acts 1:9-12	Acts 2:1-47 1 Corinthians 12:13 Ephesians 2:11-22

Months: **Nisan**—*March, April* • **Sivan**—*May, June* • **Tishri**—*September, October*

		7th Month (Tishri) Festival of Tabernacles		
	Feast of Trumpets	**Day of Atonement**	**Feast of Booths or Tabernacles**	
Interlude Between Festivals	*Trumpet blown — a holy convocation*	*Atonement shall be made to cleanse you* Lev. 16:30	*Harvest celebration memorial of tabernacles in wilderness*	
	7th month, 1st day Leviticus 23:23-25	7th month, 10th day Leviticus 23:26-32	7th month, 15th day for 7 days, 8th day, Holy Convocation Leviticus 23:33-44	
	Regathering of Israel in preparation for final day of atonement Jeremiah 32:37-41	**Israel will repent and look to Messiah in one day** Zechariah 3:9, 10 12:10; 13:1; 14:9	**Families of the earth will come to Jerusalem to celebrate the Feast of Booths** Zechariah 14:16-19	**New heaven and new earth** **God tabernacles with men** Revelation 21:1-3
		Coming of Christ 		
	Ezekiel 36:24	Ezekiel 36:25-27 Hebrews 9, 10 Romans 11:25-29	Ezekiel 36:28	

Israel had two harvests each year—spring and autumn

Bound by Your Humanity— Or Unleashed by His Spirit?

DAY ONE

Read Acts 3 and mark any of the key words listed on your bookmark that are used in this chapter.

As you mark each key word or phrase, don't simply color it; think about what you learn from the text about that key word or phrase.

DAY TWO

Today, read Acts 3 again. However, this time watch where the events in this chapter take place. Although at this point you are not studying geographical locations, you might want to underline these in green (as you should all of the geographical locations in Acts). Also mark any references to *Jesus Christ (Christ)*.

Look at the diagram of the temple mount (pages 38 and 39). Locate the places where this event is occurring. This will give you a better visual picture of these events.

As you read Acts 3:11-26, note to whom Peter is speaking. What is the nationality of these people? Many times, depending on the context of what I am studying, I will mark all the references to the people of Israel, the Jews, with a dark blue star like this ✡ .

THE TEMPLE MOUNT

During the Second Temple Period

1. Second Temple (*Herod's*)
2. Western Wall
3. Wilson's Arch*
4. Barclay's Gate*
5. Small Shops
6. Main N-S Street
7. Robinson's Arch*
8. Upper City

9. Royal Porch
10. Pilasters
11. Double Gate
12. Triple Gate
13. Plaza
14. Ritual Bathhouse
15. Council House
16. Herodian Tower

17. Largest Ashlars
18. Antonia Fortress
19. Warren's Gate*
20. Court of the Gentiles
21. Eastern Gate
    or Gate Beautiful
22. Solomon's Portico

*Named after nineteenth-century explorers

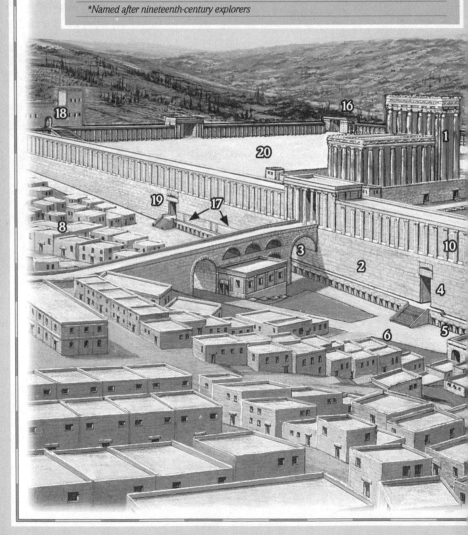

How does Peter deal with his people? What does he want them to know? If you will take careful notice, you can learn much about being Jesus' witnesses to Jews and to Gentiles.

In your notebook, set aside several pages to record the things you learn about Jesus Christ and what His witnesses share about Him when they speak to others. Record your insights from Acts 3. (When you have time, go back and do the same thing from Acts 2.)

As you make your list, remember where the witnesses got the power to speak so boldly. Do you have that same power? Are you being His witness?

DAY THREE

Read Acts 4:1-31. Note where this chapter opens and how it relates to Acts 3. Mark the key words from your bookmark used in this chapter. Don't forget to stop and think about what you are learning by marking these words.

Add to the list you have begun anything you learn about the Holy Spirit and what happens when He fills people.

DAY FOUR

Today we are going to divide Acts 4:1-31 into two segments and look at each one separately.

First read Acts 4:1-12. Examine what is happening in the light of the 5 W's and an H. Note who comes on the scene at this point, why they are there, who and what they are dealing with, and what the result is. Note what Peter says and his relationship to the Holy Spirit as he says what he does.

Once again mark every reference to Jesus Christ (Jesus) and record what you learn.

Now read Acts 4:13-31.

Add *the word of God (Thy word,* [11] *the word of the Lord)* to your bookmark. I mark references to the Word of God with a green diagram like this: Word .

Continue to mark Jesus Christ and record your insights in your notebook. Note whose hand and whose purpose predestined the events in Jesus' life.

Carefully observe how Peter and John respond. Watch how they handle themselves, what they say, how they pray, their relationship to the Holy Spirit, their determination, etc. Make a list in your notebook outlining what you learn about them: their behavior, their response, and their resolution.

DAY FIVE

Read Acts 4:32–5:11. Mark any key words or phrases from your bookmark.

Then in your notebook, list what you learn about the early church. What was this congregation of believers like? What did they do? How did they respond to one another? Compare all you see with Acts 2:41-47.

Also watch how the church and God deal with sin. What effect does the way it is dealt with have on the church?

DAY SIX

Read Acts 5:12-42 and once again mark any key words that are on your bookmark. Add to your list on the Holy Spirit what you learn from marking the references. As you mark the occurrence of the words *witnesses* or *witness*, remember to watch for synonyms because the words may not be used specifically. You will see how the people witnessed, and you should mark each

----

[11]NIV; NKJV: *your word*

instance. For example, look at Acts 5:42: "They kept right on teaching and preaching[12] Jesus as the Christ." Mark *teaching and preaching* the same way as *witnesses*. Note where they are.

As you read, it is important to keep asking the 5 W's and an H. Note who the main characters are in this segment of Acts 5, where they are, what they are doing, what the response is, why the response, what happens, how they handle themselves, what they proclaim, how they proclaim it, and why.

Also note what the apostles endure and why. From this point on in the book, mark all references to *suffering (suffer)*. Be sure to put these words on your bookmark. I mark these references with red flames like this   suffer   because I don't want to forget that it was not only given to me to believe on Jesus' name, but also to suffer for His name's sake (Philippians 1:27-30).

As you bring this week to a close, be sure to record the chapter themes for Acts 3, 4, and 5 on the ACTS AT A GLANCE chart.

DAY SEVEN

Store in your heart: Acts 4:12; 4:19,20; or 4:29.
Read and discuss: Acts 4:13-31; Acts 2:42-47; 4:32-35.

OPTIONAL QUESTIONS FOR DISCUSSION

∾ What did you learn about Peter and John from Acts 4:13? What was it about them that made them effective in the work of God? Discuss what you learned about them from chapters 3–5.

---

[12]NIV: proclaiming

   a. What was the message they proclaimed? What were the elements of their message?

   b. What were they convinced of?

   c. How did they handle the Word of God?

   d. What place did prayer have in their lives? How do you know? How did they pray? What did they pray about?

   e. How did they handle opposition? Where did their opposition come from?

   f. To what degree did they suffer? How did they handle their suffering?

ॐ What do you learn about the early church from Acts 2 and 4?

   a. What were the various activities of the church?

   b. How did these people come to know the Lord? What brought them into the church? What kind of a message did they hear? What response did this message cause?

   c. According to Acts 5:1-11, how zealous were God and the leaders of the church for the purity of the church? What effect did this have on others?

   d. How applicable do you think the activities, actions, and behavior of the early believers are to the church today?

ॐ Out of all you have read and studied this week, what spoke to you the most and why?

THOUGHT FOR THE WEEK

In all the busyness of life, in all the busyness for God, have you strayed from what God intended for you as His child, His witness? Have you forgotten that piercing precept in Zechariah 4:6: "This is the word of the LORD . . . 'Not by might nor by power, but by My Spirit,' says the LORD of hosts"?

Are you bound in your own human efforts or have you been unleashed by the Holy Spirit to do the work of God? Only the Spirit of God can do the work of God!

You cannot excuse yourself from the call to be His witnesses. You cannot say you are unlearned or untrained. You cannot say you don't have time to spend with Jesus. You have time for what is important to you. And if you say that you don't have time, you are deceiving yourself. You make time for the things that are essential or important to you, just as I do. How essential, how important, is Jesus to you?

Maybe if the church would return to its first love—all members loving God with all their heart, soul, mind, and strength and others as themselves—loving not in word only but also in deed, then we would see God adding thousands to the church in the same way as the early church experienced.

Think on these things, Beloved.

Do You Know God's Priorities?

Day One

Read Acts 6 and mark any of the key words listed on your bookmark that you see in the text.

When you finish, note the two main events covered in this chapter and how each relates to the other. Record your observations in your notebook.

Day Two

Read Acts 6:1-7 again. This time as you read, ask the 5 W's and an H of the text. In your notebook, write your observations. Note what the situation is, who is involved, how it is resolved, and why it is resolved the way it is.

Watch who does the selecting of the seven men, what qualifications they are looking for, and what is done with them when they are found. Then note the result.

What can you learn from all this for your own life?

Day Three

Read Acts 6:8–7:60 to get a broad overview of what happens to Stephen and how he handles himself.

DAY FOUR

Read Acts 6 again. This time focus on Stephen. Ask the 5 W's and an H about Stephen and record your insights in your notebook.

The "Council" referred to in Acts and the Gospels is the Sanhedrin. It was presided over by the high priest and was composed of 71 men, both Sadducees and Pharisees. It was before this body, which governed the Jews under the authority of Rome, that Stephen was brought.

Now read Acts 7:1-19. Keep in mind what the Council is accusing Stephen of. Thinking of this accusation as you read will help you understand why Stephen says what he does. Although in today's assignment you will observe all that Stephen says, be careful also to observe what you learn about the children of Israel, the patriarchs, and Joseph. This account gives a wonderful synopsis of Israel's history.

DAY FIVE

Today, continue observing the account of Stephen's witness. Read Acts 7:17-50. Note who the central figure is in this portion of Israel's history and take note of what you learn about him. However, also watch what you learn about the "fathers" and the children of Israel and how they lived and responded during this time.

As you read, you might find it profitable to color every reference to the fathers and the children of Israel in one color, and every reference to Moses in another.

DAY SIX

Read Acts 6:12–7:2a and 7:51-60. Mark any key words listed on your bookmark and used in the text. Watch for any synonyms that would refer to prayer; for example, mark *cried out* in the way you mark the word *prayer*.

Also underline or mark every reference to the men of the Council[13] in a distinctive way or color. (You will see numerous pronouns used to refer to them.) Then in your notebook jot down what you learn about these men.

Add to your list what you learn about Stephen from this final segment in Acts 7.

Record the main themes for Acts 6 and 7 on your ACTS AT A GLANCE chart.

DAY SEVEN

Store in your heart: Acts 6:4.
Read and discuss: Acts 6:1-6; 7:51-60.

OPTIONAL QUESTIONS FOR DISCUSSION

When you read Acts 6:1-6, what do you see as priorities for Christian leaders?

---

[13]NIV: *the Sanhedrin*

    a. Why do you think these are priorities? What verses do you know in the Word of God that would support these as priorities or show why they are priorities? Share them.

    b. What was the conflict that arose?

    c. How was the conflict handled?

    d. What kind of men were to be selected?

    e. Who was responsible for their selection?

    f. What was done once they were selected?

∾ What did you learn about Stephen from your study this week?

∾ How wise was the congregation's selection of Stephen? How do you know?

∾ What are the priorities for the leaders of your church or congregation?

    a. How are these priorities set forth?

    b. What does your congregation see as the priorities for your pastor, minister, priest, elders, or congregational leaders?

    c. What kind of assistance is provided for the leadership of your church?

    d. What are the qualifications in your church for these men, for your elders, for your deacons? Is there any consideration given to 1 Timothy 3?

∾ What did you learn about the Jewish leaders, the members of the Council that was ruling Israel under the Romans?

∾ As you look at the contrast between the elders and deacons, the apostles, the congregation, and the Council, what have you learned about how the church and its members should function?

THOUGHT FOR THE WEEK

How important it is, Beloved, that you realize that the foundation for all that you are and do is the Word of God. Even prayer must be based on the Word of God. In John 15:7, Jesus says that if you abide in Him and His words abide in you, then you shall ask what you will and it will be done for you.

But the Word of God alone is not enough. That is God's communication to you, but you must also communicate with Him. Christianity is a relationship. Prayer and the Word of God maintain and sustain that relationship.

Therefore, no matter what transpires in your life or in the life of your church, you must not neglect prayer and the Word of God. And above all, you must see to it that your leaders have adequate support from men who are full of the Spirit and wisdom, so that they can give themselves to the imperatives of prayer and the Word of God.

How can God's church run apart from prayer? How can His sheep be fed anything but the pure, unadulterated Word of God, which as John 17:17 says sanctifies them because it is truth?

Encourage and support your spiritual leaders so they have time to give themselves to prayer and the Word!

Then you be the Stephens... full of the Spirit and wisdom—a wisdom that comes because you know the Word of God and have sought in prayer the will of God so that you know what is the work of God for you.

Suffering—
It Goes with Salvation

Day One

Read Acts 8. As you read today, simply look for one key repeated word on your list: *witness*. To witness is "to proclaim Christ, preach the Word, preach the gospel, explain the Scriptures." Therefore, also mark anything that has to do with witnessing the same way you have been marking the word *witnesses*. For example, in Acts 8:4 you will want to mark *went about preaching the word*.[14]

Day Two

Read Acts 1:8; 6:5; 7:58—8:40. Then read Acts 8 and examine it in the light of the 5 W's and an H. Watch what is happening, where it is happening, and why it is happening. Note who is involved. Who are the main characters in this chapter?

Mark any other key words on your bookmark that are in chapter 8. Add the word *baptized* to your bookmark. I mark it like this: *baptized* and color it light blue. You might want to go back and mark *baptized* in Acts 1:5; 2:38,41.

---

[14]NIV: *preached the word wherever they went*
   KJV; NKJV: *went everywhere preaching the word*

DAY THREE

Read Acts 8:1-8 again and underline any references to geographical locations. Then in your notebook record where these events take place, how the people came to be in these places, and how what they did in these places became a fulfillment of Acts 1:8. Also mark any references to time. Note the phrase in Acts 8:1 *on that day*.[15] It is significant.

When you finish the above, take a good look at Philip and list the main events in Philip's journeys as recorded in Acts 8. Trace these journeys on the map (page 53).

By the way, from your Scripture readings yesterday, who do you think the Philip of Acts 8 is?

DAY FOUR

Read Acts 7:58–8:4; 9:1-31. Mark any key words that are on your list.

DAY FIVE

Read the same Scriptures as in yesterday's assignment. In your notebook list the major events in the life of Saul (Paul) as they occur in the text. Also note what God calls Paul to do, to whom He calls him, and where he goes. Observe the text carefully as this is important information.

You will find that what you learn can be a great blessing to you, because later, in 1 Corinthians 11:1, Paul writes, "Be imitators of me, just as I also am of Christ." In Philippians 3:17 he tells the church to follow his example and observe others according to the pattern they have seen in him.

---

[15]KJV; NKJV: *at that time*

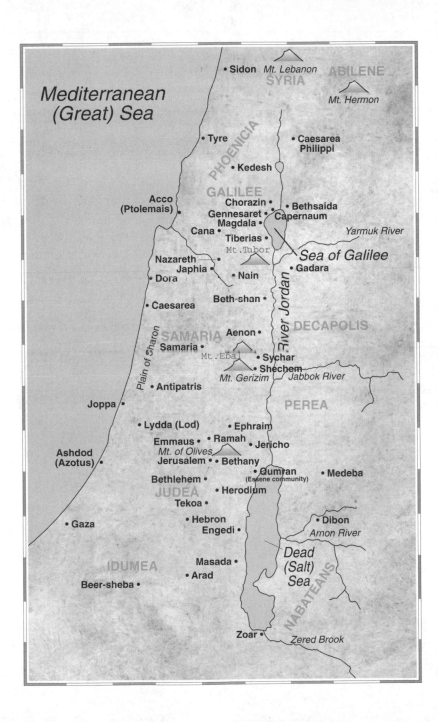

DAY SIX

We first looked at Peter and John's ministry, then Stephen's, and then Philip's, and then Saul's conversion. You may want to write the names of these men in the margin of your Bible where the text focuses on them so you can easily spot the accounts of each.

Isn't it interesting that Saul was a major force in the persecution of the church that began the day of Stephen's death? And that the persecution became God's instrument for the fulfillment of Acts 1:8—that they would be witnesses not only in Jerusalem, but in Judea and Samaria? Soon we will see how Saul was God's major force in taking the gospel beyond the land of Israel "to the remotest part of the earth," as Acts 1:8 says Jesus' followers were to do.

However, for now the text takes us back to Peter and what is going to be a most significant event, especially for those of us who were not born Jewish (of the physical seed of Abraham).

Read Acts 9:31 and notice where the church is and what it is experiencing at that point.

Now read Acts 9:32-43. Note what happens and where these events take place on the map on page 66. Also note what happens as a result of the events. Record your insights in your notebook. On page 55 you will find the chart SEQUENCE OF EVENTS IN PAUL'S LIFE AFTER HIS CONVERSION. I think you will find it a helpful reference as we progress through Acts.

Finally, record the main themes of Acts 8 and 9 on the ACTS AT A GLANCE chart.

DAY SEVEN

Store in your heart: Acts 9:15,16.

Read and discuss: Acts 7:58–8:3; 9:1-30; 1 Corinthians 15:1-11; 1 Timothy 1:15,16.

Sequence of Events in Paul's Life after His Conversion*

*There are differing opinions on these dates. For continuity's sake this chart will be the basis for dates pertaining to Paul's life.

Year A.D.	Event
33-34	Conversion, time in Damascus
35-47	Some silent years, except we know that Paul:
	1. Spent time in Arabia and Damascus
	2. Made first visit to Jerusalem
	3. Went to Tarsus, Syria-Cilicia area
	4. Was with Barnabas in Antioch
	5. With Barnabas took relief to brethren in Judea—Paul's second visit to Jerusalem
	6. Returned to Antioch; was sent out with Barnabas by church at Antioch
	First missionary journey: *Galatians written(?)*
47-48	
49	Apostolic Council at Jerusalem—Paul visits Jerusalem (compare Acts 15 with Galatians 2:1)
49-51	**Second missionary journey:** *1 and 2 Thessalonians written*
52-56	**Third missionary journey:** *1 and 2 Corinthians and Romans written*
56	Paul goes to Jerusalem and is arrested; held at Caesarea
57-59	Appearance before Felix and Drusilla; before Festus; before Agrippa
59-60	Appeals to Caesar, sent from Caesarea to Rome
60-62	First Roman imprisonment: *Ephesians, Philemon, Colossians, and Philippians written*
62	Paul's release; possible trip to Spain
62	Paul in Macedonia: *1 Timothy written*
62	Paul goes to Crete: *Titus written*
63-64	Paul taken to Rome and imprisoned: *2 Timothy written*
64	Paul is absent from the body and present with the Lord
	(Others put Paul's conversion about A.D. 35, his death in A.D. 68.)

OPTIONAL QUESTIONS FOR DISCUSSION

∾ When you compiled all you learned about Saul, what did you record as the sequence of events in Saul's life? (By the way, Saul's name was changed to Paul, and since that is how he is best known, from this point on I'll refer to him as Paul.)

   a. What did you learn about God's plan for Paul?

   b. What was Paul like when he was Saul, before he was saved on the road to Damascus? What was he like afterward?

   c. What was Paul's relationship to the Holy Spirit?

   d. How did the church respond to Paul after he was converted? Why?

   e. Who was the one who befriended Paul and took him under his care when the disciples in Jerusalem wouldn't associate with him?

∾ What are some of the practical things we can learn from Paul's life, conversion, and subsequent walk with the Lord?

∾ What do you learn from 1 Corinthians 15:1-11 and 1 Timothy 1:15,16? What do these verses tell you about the importance of our example, the way we live out our Christianity before others? Could you say what Paul said in Philippians 3:17? Should you be able to? What, if anything, would have to change? Would it be worth it?

THOUGHT FOR THE WEEK

The chief of sinners, the one who persecuted the church and put Christians to death, was to be a chosen instrument of God! Can you imagine!

O Beloved, Jesus didn't come into the world to call "the righteous." He came for sinners. He came for those who know they have sinned, for those who understand that they are not worthy of God's mercy or His favor!

It doesn't matter if you feel you are "a chief of sinners." It only matters that you avail yourself of the grace of God. Yes, it will mean suffering. Suffering is a gift that comes with salvation. Later Paul would write to the Romans that "the sufferings of this present time are not worthy to be compared with the glory that is to be revealed to us" (8:18).

Like Paul, because of the greatness of your past sin, the church may have trouble at first receiving you. Be patient. Don't be discouraged. In time people will see the genuineness of your faith, and they will stand in awe at the grace of God that labors in you for His glory as you are faithful to His call on your life.

Remember, you too are a chosen vessel. You too, if you are a child of God, have the same Holy Spirit in you in the same measure as Paul. Go forth, filled with the Spirit of God as His witness wherever He sends you.

Week Six

Baptized with the Spirit?
Who... When... How?

Day One

Read Acts 9:40–10:23. Mark any key words that are on your bookmark. Add what you learn about the Holy Spirit to the list in your notebook.

As you read this portion of Scripture, look at the map (page 53) and note where Peter is during this time. Note too where Cornelius is. Think about Peter's nationality and Cornelius' nationality. Don't read just words, but think of these men as flesh and blood. One is a "slave" of Rome; one is a commander for Rome in the Italian cohort.

Day Two

Read Acts 10:24-48. Using the list on your bookmark, mark any key words. Think about the purpose of the vision that Peter had. Write in your notebook why you think Peter had this particular vision. Then give careful attention to the message Peter gave to Cornelius. List in your notebook the main points of that message. Note what happened as a result of Peter's message and Cornelius' desire.

Next to Acts 10:44 write in the margin of your Bible "8 years after Pentecost," for this is when this incredible event took place.

DAY THREE

Read Acts 11:1-18 and mark the key words. Don't forget to list in your notebook all you observe about the Holy Spirit.

As you read Acts 11:1-18, keep in mind the 5 W's and an H. Answer these questions as you read what happens in Jerusalem as a result of Peter's visit to the home of Cornelius. You will see how significant Peter's visit was!

DAY FOUR

The events in Acts 10 and 11 are very significant in understanding the "baptism of the Spirit." Look up the following verses, read them, and carefully observe what you learn about the Holy Spirit from these passages. How do they relate to one another?

Although some of what you see will be a repeat of what we studied in Acts 1 and 2, the review will be beneficial. This is a survey course, so we may not go as deep as you would like.

However, just learning to observe the text and see what it says is absolutely invaluable. It gives you a solid foundation for interpretation and will help keep you from handling Scripture improperly. Record your insights in your notebook.

Read Acts 1:4,5,8; Acts 2:33 (this is an explanation of Pentecost); Acts 2:38,39 (note who the promise is for—those near [the Jews] and those far off, as many as the Lord shall call. These would have to be those who were not Jews but were in Samaria and from the remotest part of the earth.) As you read each passage, list in outline form exactly what the text says.

So where does the gospel go?

First it goes to Jerusalem.

Then with the stoning of Stephen and the persecution of the church, the gospel goes to Judea and Samaria (Acts 8:1-8).

What happens in Samaria? The Samaritans believe. So Peter and John go to Samaria and lay hands on them, and they too receive the Holy Spirit, for He had not yet fallen on them. However this happened, those watching could see that the Samaritans had received the Holy Spirit.

Then in Acts 10, Cornelius, a Gentile, and his household receive the Holy Spirit. How? When? Look carefully at Acts 11:17. Watch the time phrase "after"[16] and compare what you see with Ephesians 1:13. All that happens in Acts 10 is what Peter explains to the leaders in Jerusalem in Acts 11.

Read the following verses and note exactly what they say. Let Scripture interpret Scripture: Acts 10:44-48 and 11:15-18. Mark each occurrence of *just as*.[17] Also look at Acts 11:16 and

---

[16]NIV; KJV: Does not use *after*.
  NKJV: *when*
[17]NIV; NKJV: also uses *as* in 11:15
  KJV: *as well as* or *as*

note what Peter remembered. Compare what you saw in the Gospels (Matthew 3:11; Mark 1:8; Luke 3:16; John 1:33).

From all that you have seen in your study of Acts, what is the Word teaching us about "the baptism of the Holy Spirit"? According to the Word of God, is the baptism of the Holy Spirit a part of salvation?

DAY FIVE

Read Acts 11:19-30. Note what happens now with respect to where the gospel is being preached and to those who are responding.

Mark any key words. Also underline the geographical references and mark time phrases.

DAY SIX

Read Acts 12. Mark your key words. Note who the focus is on in this chapter. Watch the events of this chapter. Examine them in the light of the 5 W's and an H. Record your insights in your notebook.

Record the themes of Acts 10, 11, and 12 on the ACTS AT A GLANCE chart.

DAY SEVEN

Store in your heart: Acts 10:15 and/or Acts 10:34,35. Read and discuss: Acts 11:1-18.

OPTIONAL QUESTIONS FOR DISCUSSION

What kind of a message did Peter bring to Cornelius and his household? How did Cornelius respond?

ᵔᵕ When you did your assignment on Acts 10 and 11, what did you learn from observing the text about the baptism of the Holy Spirit? Explain your insights by taking others in your group to the text of Scripture and proving your point from the Word of God rather than from experience. This exercise is not to invalidate anyone's experience; rather it is to bring all your experiences to the Word of God so that it can validate them or show you where your terminology may not be in accord with the clear teaching of the Word.

Remember, the Word of God is the plumbline that shows us what is true and what is not.

ᵔᵕ How does what you have seen in Acts fit with 1 Corinthians 12:13? By the way, the prepositions "in" and "with" when it speaks of the baptism of the Spirit is one and the same in the Greek. The word is *en* and can be translated "in," "with," or "by."

The terms "by one Spirit . . . baptized," "baptized in," "baptized with," or "baptized by" the Spirit are used only seven times in Scripture: Matthew 3:11; Mark 1:8; Luke 3:16; John 1:33; Acts 1:5; Acts 11:16; and 1 Corinthians 12:13.

The promise of the Spirit is in Luke 24:49; Acts 1:4; Acts 2:33,39; Galatians 3:14,17; Ephesians 1:13,14; Ephesians 2:12; Hebrews 9:15; and Hebrews 11:39.

In three places you see Peter involved with people receiving the gift of the Holy Spirit: Acts 2; Acts 8:4-17; and Acts 10:44-48.

ᵔᵕ What else have you learned from these first 11 chapters of Acts about the Holy Spirit and His relationship and working in the life of the believer? Share your insights from your notebook.

THOUGHT FOR THE WEEK

Now, Beloved, if you are a true child of God, have you been baptized by the Holy Spirit? Then the Spirit of God is in you in all His fulness.

What is your responsibility? It is stated in Ephesians 5:18-20: "Do not get drunk with wine, for that is dissipation [being out of control], but be filled with the Spirit, speaking to one another in psalms and hymns and spiritual songs, singing and making melody with your heart to the Lord; always giving thanks for all things in the name of our Lord Jesus Christ to God, even the Father."

The verb "be filled" is in the present imperative tense, which means that God is commanding you to be habitually filled with the Spirit. If you are a child of God, you have the Spirit of God; now don't quench the Spirit. Be filled continuously, and watch what happens, Beloved, as you walk by the Spirit.

Don't Know What to Do?
Try Prayer and Fasting

DAY ONE

Read Acts 12:24–13:41. Mark any key words that are on your bookmark.

Then add what you learn about the Holy Spirit to your list in your notebook.

DAY TWO

Acts 13 marks the beginning of Paul's first missionary journey. Therefore, the locations where Paul goes are very important. Read through Acts 13:1-41 and underline every geographical location. Then on the map (page 66) titled PAUL'S FIRST MISSIONARY JOURNEY, trace where Paul goes on this journey. Tracing this part of his journey will be extremely profitable. (Remember that where Paul traveled is modern-day Turkey.)

DAY THREE

Read Acts 13:42-52 and once again mark the key words and phrases. Mark all the references to *eternal life*[18] *(salvation)*.

---

[18]KJV; NKJV: also uses *everlasting life*

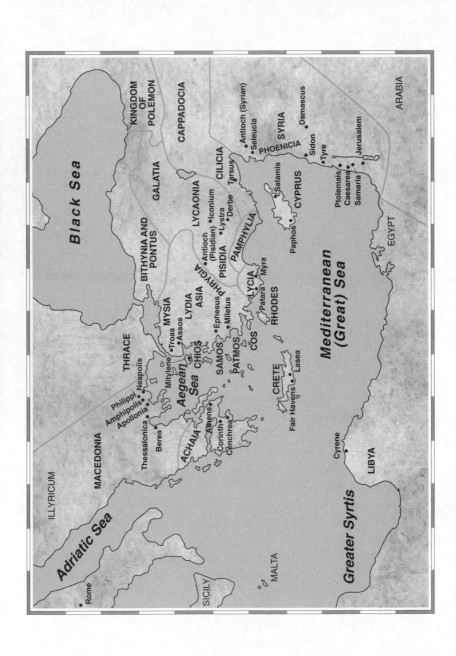

Then look up the following references in Acts where the word *saved* is used and mark it in the same way you marked *eternal life* and *salvation*: Acts 2:21,40,47; 4:12; 11:14; 15:1,11; 16:30,31. Make a list of all that you learn about being saved. Then in your notebook write down what you learn about eternal life.

Also continue to mark any geographical locations as you trace Paul's journey on the map.

DAY FOUR

Read Acts 14:1-20. Mark any key repeated words. Also mark the geographical references and then trace them on the map.

DAY FIVE

Read Acts 14:21-28. Again mark key words and geographical locations. Continue to trace Paul's missionary journey. Acts 14 brings Paul's missionary journey to an end.

DAY SIX

Today you need to go back through Acts 13 and 14 and note what happens in each major city where Paul spends time. Note what he does when he reaches each city, how he approaches the people, the message that he brings, and the end result. You can learn so much about being God's witness from Paul's life. Record your facts either in the margin of your Bible or in your notebook.

Record the themes of Acts 13 and 14 on the ACTS AT A GLANCE chart.

DAY SEVEN

📖 Store in your heart: Acts 13:2.
Read and discuss: Acts 13:1-5,15-41.

OPTIONAL QUESTIONS FOR DISCUSSION

∾ What do you learn from Acts 13:1-5 about the place of prayer and fasting in the church? Do you see any relationship between these disciplines and the ministry of the Holy Spirit? What do you think would happen if we gave more time to ministering to the Lord in prayer and fasting? Would it make us more sensitive to the Lord's calling of people for His work?

∾ Have you ever prayed and fasted? Will you share why you prayed and fasted and what happened as a result?

∾ What was Paul's strategy when he went into a city? Where did he begin? Was Paul's message always received? When it wasn't, was it because Paul wasn't filled with the Spirit? According to what you saw about salvation and eternal life, who believed?

∾ What were the elements of Paul's message when he delivered the gospel?

∾ According to Acts 13:37-39, why was the resurrection important? What did it show?

∾ Under what circumstances did Paul preach the gospel? What did it cost him? What can we learn that we can apply to our own lives?

∾ What has spoken to you the most from your study this week? What did you see that you can apply to your life?

THOUGHT FOR THE WEEK

Oh, how you—how I—need to learn the disciplines of ministering to the Lord in prayer and fasting. When we learn to sit at His feet, to seek His face, to wait upon Him, then we will know what He wants us to do.

Throughout the book of Acts, people pray and God moves in answer to their prayers. The Word is proclaimed, and people are saved. Or people resist the work of the Word and the Spirit even though their hearts are cut to the quick. Behind all this is the blessed Holy Spirit of God, filling, leading, directing, comforting, and speaking.

O Beloved, may you learn to walk in total dependence upon the Spirit, seeking His will, not yours; His way, not yours; His timing, not yours; His power, not yours; His wisdom, not yours . . . may you keep on being filled with the Spirit!

Not Perfect . . . but Faithful

Day One

Read Acts 14:26-28 and compare it with Acts 13:1-4. Where did Paul's first missionary journey begin and end?

Now read Acts 15:1-35. As you read, note where Paul is, who is with him, where they go, and why.

Day Two

Read Acts 14:26–15:35 again. This time mark any key words from your bookmark.

Mark the word *Gentiles* and any pronouns that refer to the Gentiles, but don't add it to your bookmark. This word is used throughout the book of Acts, but it is key only in this passage. Therefore, you will not want to continue marking it.

Also mark the word *grace*. When you mark *grace*, also mark any reference to *the Law of Moses (custom of Moses,* [19] *Moses . . . is read in the synagogues*[20]). I usually mark *law* this way 📖 .

---

[19]NIV: *custom taught by Moses*
  KJV: *after the manner of Moses*
[20]KJV; NKJV: *being read in the synagogues*

DAY THREE

Today go through Acts 15 and list everything you learned yesterday from marking the word *Gentiles* and its pronouns. As you do, ask the 5 W's and an H to learn all you can about how the church fathers in Jerusalem dealt with this situation.

What do you learn about the place of circumcision and the law in the life of a convert to Christianity?

What were the converts instructed to do? Record this in your notebook.

DAY FOUR

Read Acts 15:30-41. Notice where Paul and Barnabas are and the names of those who are with them. Then observe what Paul wants to do and what happens as a result.

When you finish, read 2 Timothy 4:11. This is Paul's last epistle to his son in the faith, Timothy. Note what he writes about Mark, who is called John Mark in Acts 15.

What do you learn from or about Barnabas in this account? Look up the following passages where Barnabas is mentioned: Acts 4:36,37; 9:27; 11:22-30; 12:25; 13:1,2,7,42-51; 1 Corinthians 9:6; Galatians 2:1,9,13; Colossians 4:10. Record everything you observe about Barnabas. Watch for anything that would show you his relationship to Mark (John Mark).

You may want to write these cross-references on Barnabas in the margin of your Bible next to one of the Acts references.

DAY FIVE

Paul begins his second missionary journey in Acts 15:39. This is an important time in Paul's life because it is during this time that he meets Timothy. There is a map on page 73 for you to trace this journey. You will remember his course better

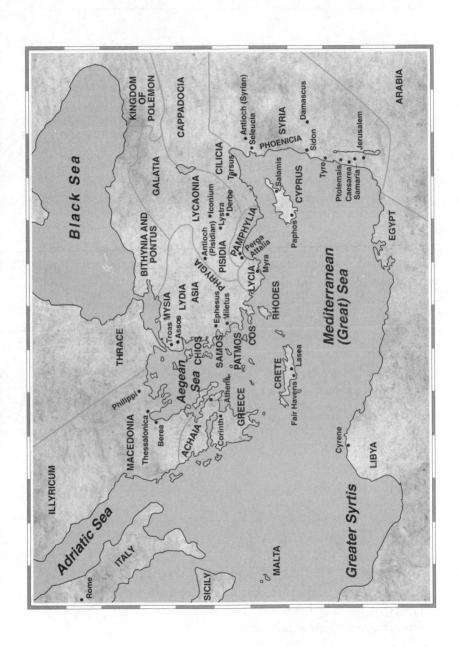

if you mark it yourself, rather than simply looking at a map that has it traced for you.

Read through Acts 15:39–16:12. Underline every geographical location Paul visits and then trace his path on the map.

Finally, record in your notebook all you learn from the text about Timothy.

DAY SIX

Read Acts 16:11-40. Mark any key words from your bookmark. Mark any references that refer to the enemy or any of his demonic spirits. I mark references to the enemy with a red pitchfork like this Satan .

When you finish, list in your notebook the main events that occur in this chapter, and who responds to the gospel and under what circumstances.

Also observe how Paul and Silas handle the various situations they encounter. There are valuable lessons in all this for us.

Don't forget to record your chapter themes for Acts 15 and 16 on the ACTS AT A GLANCE chart.

DAY SEVEN

Store in your heart: Acts 16:30,31.

Read and discuss: Acts 16:1-3; 1 Corinthians 4:14-17; 1 Timothy 1:1,2,18-20; 4:12-16; 5:21-23; 6:11,12; 2 Timothy 1:1-8; 2:1-3; 3:10-12; 4:1-9. (As you read these verses about Timothy, make a list outlining all you learn about Paul and Timothy and their relationship.)

OPTIONAL QUESTIONS FOR DISCUSSION

∾ As suggested under "Read and discuss," read the passages one by one. What do you learn from each passage about Timothy and about Paul's relationship to Timothy? From these passages, what do you discern as Paul's concerns for Timothy? (It would be good to list these on a visual aid if you have one.)

∾ How important was Paul's relationship with Timothy with respect to the gospel? Why?

∾ Who was the last person Paul ever communicated with, and what was his concern?

∾ What do you learn from this relationship? What did Paul model for Timothy? How do you think Paul and Timothy's relationship fit with Jesus' command in Matthew 28:18-20?

∾ What was Paul urging Timothy to do in 2 Timothy 2:1-3? Do you have a relationship like this with another believer? Who are you raising up in the gospel for the furtherance of the kingdom?

THOUGHT FOR THE WEEK

Who have you nurtured in the gospel of Jesus Christ? Is there a faithful man, a faithful woman, you can take under your wing and instruct in the truths and ways of the Lord?

Who has been close enough to you to see the way you live? Who has followed your teaching, conduct, purpose, faith, patience, love, perseverance, persecutions, and sufferings? Or are these things woefully lacking in your life, so that you cannot say with Holy Spirit boldness that anyone should follow you?

Christendom desperately needs godly role models. Not men and women who the world thinks are perfect and never make mistakes. Paul wasn't perfect! Even Paul and Barnabas had a falling-out. But Paul pressed on. He knew that he had not obtained it (Philippians 3:12), but he pressed on toward the prize of the high calling of God in Christ Jesus. And because he pressed on, he could say, "Follow my pattern. Be an imitator of me, as I am of Christ Jesus."

Whatever is necessary, Beloved, you need to do it so that you too can say to your "Timothy": "Join with me in suffering for the gospel of Jesus Christ. I have fought the good fight. I have finished the course. I have kept the faith. . . ."

Then you can pass the baton on to your faithful son or daughter in the gospel, and the work of the kingdom will continue until He comes.

Is Your Heart Grieved by the Idols People Worship?

DAY ONE

Read Acts 17:1-10. Mark the key words on your bookmark. Then examine Paul's time in Thessalonica in the light of the 5 W's and an H. In your notebook or in the margin of your Bible, write where Paul is and list anything significant that you want to remember about his time in this city.

Make sure you note how long Paul stayed there, how he approached and dealt with the people, and what happened as a result of his visit.

Trace Paul's course of travel as given to you in Acts 17:1 on the map of Paul's second missionary journey (page 73).

DAY TWO

First Thessalonians 1:1–2:12 will give you further insight into what made Paul's visit in Thessalonica so successful despite the persecution he suffered.

It will also give you some wonderful Scriptures to pray back to the Lord. I often find myself praying 1 Thessalonians 1:5 and examining my relationship to people in the light of 1 Thessalonians 2:1-12. I pray that studying this passage will be an encouragement to you. Record any LFL you see. (Remember in your instructions in the front of the book, we talked about "Lessons for Life.")

You might want to cross-reference Acts 17:1-9 and 1 Thessalonians 1:1–2:12 in your Bible. When there are only two Scriptures you want to cross-reference, you can write each by the other in the margin of your Bible. That way, as in this instance, you always have the cross-reference to the other passage.

DAY THREE

Read Acts 17:10-34 and mark key words. Then carefully examine what happened in Berea and in Athens and record your insights in your notebook.

Notice how Paul is received in each of these places and how he deals with the people. Also keep in mind who is with Paul on these journeys.

Watch what provokes Paul's spirit. When you look at our society or visit various cities or countries, is your spirit provoked? Often provocation becomes a call to prayer. Never underestimate the power of your prayers!

Don't forget to record Paul's journeys on the map (page 73).

DAY FOUR

Read Acts 18:1-18. Mark the key words. Note what happens when Paul arrives in Corinth and what he does until Silas and Timothy arrive. Note whom he meets and who continues with him on his journey. Record your observations in your notebook. Priscilla and Aquila become important figures in the work of the kingdom.

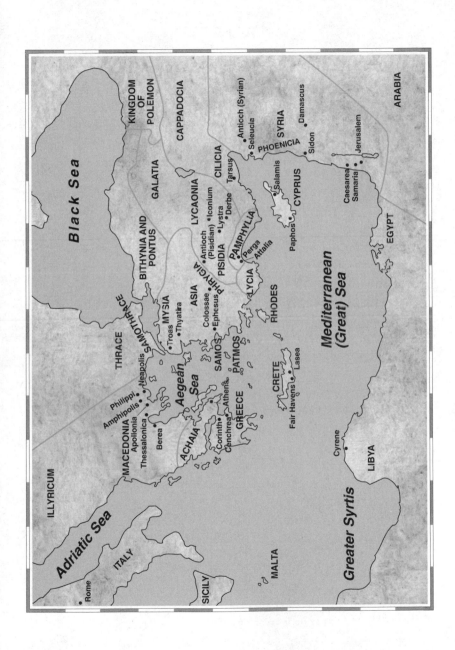

DAY FIVE

Read Acts 18:1-28. Trace Paul's journey back to Antioch on the map (page 73). Note what Paul does in Ephesus.

In Acts 18:23, Paul begins his third missionary journey. Therefore as you underline the various cities Paul visits, trace these on the map, PAUL'S THIRD MISSIONARY JOURNEY (page 79). Note what Paul is doing on this journey.

In Acts 18:24-28, note who the focus is on at this point and the role Priscilla and Aquila play in his life.

Read 1 Corinthians 16:19; Romans 16:3-5; and 2 Timothy 4:19 and note what you learn about Priscilla and Aquila from these verses.

As you study these references, look also at the chart SEQUENCE OF EVENTS IN PAUL'S LIFE AFTER HIS CONVERSION (page 55) and note when and where they were when Paul wrote that particular epistle or where they are when Paul refers to them. What are they doing?

DAY SIX

Read Acts 19 and mark key words. Mark any references to the Way.[21] Go back to Acts 9:2 and mark the references[22] there also. Be sure not to confuse the Way with the modern religious group who call themselves "The Way." The use of the term in the book of Acts referred to Christian believers. Also compare Acts 19:9 to John 14:6.

Record in your notebook what you learn from marking Holy Spirit.[23]

---

[21]KJV: that way
[22]KJV: this way
[23]KJV: Holy Ghost

As you study all that transpires in Ephesus, remember that Paul spent a short time there (Acts 18:18-21) and left Priscilla and Aquila there. Then Apollos came to Ephesus.

Now Paul is on his third missionary journey, strengthening the disciples. Note how long Paul stays in Ephesus and all that happens during that time.

Remember to record the themes for chapters 17, 18, and 19 on the ACTS AT A GLANCE chart.

DAY SEVEN

Store in your heart: Acts 17:30,31.

Read and discuss: Acts 17:30,31; Acts 18:19-21; and Acts 19:1-19.

OPTIONAL QUESTIONS FOR DISCUSSION

∾ Review what you learn about Paul's first visit to Ephesus and then Apollos' visit there.

∾ When Paul arrived in Ephesus the second time, had the people there received the Holy Spirit? What did they know about? What were they ignorant of?

∾ What happened as a result when Paul laid hands upon these men? To how many men did this happen?

∾ Apart from 1 Corinthians 12–14, speaking in tongues is mentioned in only three events in the book of Acts. Look up each of these occurrences and note what happened each time, to whom, and why (if the text tells you): Acts 2:4,11; 10:46; 19:6.

∾ Remember the word *repentance* means to have a change of mind. When you study Acts 19, do you see repentance— not the word, but the act? Where and how? What does this show you about the effect of the gospel in Ephesus?

ↄ As you have watched Paul on these three missionary journeys, what have you learned from him about sharing the
   gospel? What have you learned from his life about the
   consequences of being Jesus' witness? Is it always easy?

ↄ What were some of the problems and persecutions Paul
   endured because of his obedience to the faith?

ↄ Can you relate to Paul in any way? How?

THOUGHT FOR THE WEEK

Someday God is going to judge the world in righteousness.
And it will be in righteousness because the gospel will go out to
the ends of the earth. God is not willing that any person
perish. He wants all people everywhere to be saved. Therefore, if anyone longs to know the truth about God, God will see
that he hears it. Yet not all who hear will be saved, simply
because they won't change their mind when they are con-
fronted with truth.

The whole city of Ephesus had the opportunity to believe.
Paul was in that city for two years (Acts 19:10). Men bound by
Satan were set free. Other people were healed. Bonfires lit the
city skies as people brought their evil books and burned them.
Those of "the Way" caused a great disturbance, so the people
were well aware of the gospel Paul preached. Yet most preferred
Artemis (Diana), the many-breasted statue crafted by the
hands of men, to the living God who gives life and breath to all
things. They preferred the myth of a goddess who had fallen
from the sky to the truth of the One who sent the Son of Man
from heaven to die for their sins and rise from the dead that
they might live forever.

O Beloved, when you see the idols of men, may you too be
grieved in your heart. For unless people repent, they will perish.

But how will they know this unless someone tells them?
And who will tell them . . . no matter the cost?

Will You Declare the Truth—
No Matter the Cost?

DAY ONE

Read Acts 20:1-16. Note where Paul is, where he goes, where he is headed and why. Trace his travels on the map (page 79) that covers his third missionary journey. Mark time phrases and any key words.

DAY TWO

Read Acts 20:17-38. As you do, catch the spirit, the emotion, the intensity of this situation. Don't rush through this passage. Read it, think about what you read, and then read it again. Ask God to speak to your heart as you hear and see Paul's concern for these people. Remember, Paul is instrumental in their lives and their birth into the kingdom of God.

DAY THREE

Read Acts 20:17-38 again. This time mark key repeated words. Don't forget to write in your notebook what you learn about the Holy Spirit of God.

Also record in your notebook what you learn from this passage about Paul, his ministry, and his message.

What do you see from this passage that is so important for the servant of God?

Was Paul loved by everyone? Was he loved by the elders at Ephesus? What was important?

DAY FOUR

Read Acts 21:1-14. Mark every reference to geographical locations and record these on the map (page 79) on which you are tracing Paul's third missionary journey.

Also mark any key words or phrases.

DAY FIVE

As you read the two passages mentioned in today's study, be sure to mark any key words.

Paul's third missionary journey is about finished. Read Acts 21:15-17 and bring it to its end on the map (page 79).

Now read Acts 21:17-26. What was the problem Paul faced when he entered Jerusalem? Record it in your notebook. Do you think Paul ever wearied from all the conflicts which he endured?

Did he quit?

DAY SIX

Read Acts 21:26-40. If you see any key words or phrases, mark them.

In your notebook, record the accusations they were making against Paul and the effect it had on the city.

On the diagram of the temple mount (pages 38 and 39), note where the Antonia fortress was located in relation to the temple. This is where Jesus was brought by Pilate before the multitude.

The elevation of this fortress enabled the Roman soldiers to keep watch over the temple mount area. They were right there to quell any disturbance. Note the mob reaction in this account. Then watch how the Roman soldiers get involved and what happens as a result.

Record the themes of chapters 20 and 21 on the AT A GLANCE chart.

DAY SEVEN

Store in your heart: Acts 20:26,27.

Read and discuss: Acts 9:15,16; 20:17-38; 21:8-14; 2 Timothy 1:8-12.

OPTIONAL QUESTIONS FOR DISCUSSION

∞ To whom is Paul speaking in Acts 20:17-38? Why?

∞ What do you learn from this passage about Paul's ministry while he was in Ephesus?

   a. What did Paul teach?

   b. Where did Paul teach and minister?

   c. How did Paul minister? What did he model before others?

∞ What awaited Paul? How did he know that? What different ways had he been shown that bonds and afflictions awaited him?

∞ What effect did this difficult word about his future have on Paul? Why do you think he responded the way he did?

∞ Some people say that Paul was wrong to go to Jerusalem when he had been warned about what awaited him. How would you deal with that statement in the light of the Word of God?

∞ What do you learn about Paul's commitment from these passages? What do you learn about his life and ministry?

∾ What was Paul's concern for the church at Ephesus?

∾ Do you think it was a valid concern? Should that be our concern today?

∾ What do you learn from Acts 20:17-38 about the word of His grace?

∾ What do you see happening in your life as a result of doing this study in Acts? Is the "word of His grace" having an effect on your life? Share how. Be as specific as you can.

THOUGHT FOR THE WEEK

Faith is not faith until it is tested. Paul had been told from the very beginning of his life in Christ that he would suffer for the sake of the name of his Lord. Suffer he had, and yet more awaited him. But he was not deterred from doing the will of God; he would not stop the work of God. His course was set, and that course would take him through many trials and afflictions.

Paul knew God's calling upon his life. He had been appointed a preacher and an apostle and a teacher, and because of that he would suffer.

And suffer he did—*but* he was not ashamed. Why? Because he knew whom he had believed, and he was convinced that God was able to guard all that he had entrusted to Him. Paul's eyes were not on today, but tomorrow; not on the temporal, but the eternal.

Paul had also guarded the treasure that had been entrusted to him. He had not only proclaimed the gospel; he lived it.

What about you and me, Beloved? Is there not a calling upon our lives also? Haven't we been told that in this world we are going to suffer tribulation, that all who live godly in Christ Jesus will suffer persecution? Of course!

Are we going to turn back, to not declare truth if it costs us our freedom? How dare we! How will we ever face our Lord without shame? How will we look Paul in the face in eternity, when he was our example of what it meant to be a follower of our Lord?

O Beloved, may we learn the whole counsel of God. May we share it. May we live it no matter what awaits us.

I commend you to God and to the Word of His grace, which is able to build you up and to give you the inheritance among all those who are sanctified. Stay in His Word. . . .

Bold and Confident
Because of the Spirit

DAY ONE

Simply read Acts 21:27–22:30. Don't look for or mark anything this first time around. Just catch the mood of what is happening.

Watch how Paul handles himself.

DAY TWO

Read through Acts 22 again today. This time mark any key words on your bookmark. Also in this chapter mark the word *appointed*.[24]

In your notebook list the details of Paul's conversion experience. Observe how Paul conducts himself with the Roman commander, the Jewish mob, and then the Roman centurion.

DAY THREE

Today, go back and read the account of Paul's conversion as recorded in Acts 9:1-31. Then compare this account with

---

[24]NIV: *assigned, chosen*
  KJV; NKJV: also uses *chosen*

what Paul shares with the Jewish mob in Acts 22. Understanding both these passages will help fill in some of the details regarding Paul's conversion. Add the details to the list in your notebook or reconstruct again the complete scenario.

DAY FOUR

Read Acts 22:30–23:35. Don't mark anything today. Once again simply catch all that is going on and the intensity with which these men are coming against Paul. What does this intensity tell you about the effectiveness of Paul's ministry?

Remember, the Council is the Sanhedrin, that Jewish body of men who ruled under Rome's authority over their own people.

DAY FIVE

Now read Acts 23 again. This time mark any key words on your bookmark. Also list in your notebook the various people who are mentioned in this chapter and what you learn about each of them from Acts 23.

DAY SIX

Read Acts 23 one more time. This time note how Paul deals with the various people mentioned in this chapter. Record your insights in your notebook. Also watch how God ministers to and protects Paul. What encouragement do you receive from this? Do you think God did this only because Paul was special to Him?

Take courage, Beloved, you are loved as much as Paul. Listen to God in the midst of your trial. He will speak to you in that still small voice of the Holy Spirit. God is the same yesterday, today, and forever.

Record the themes for Acts 22 and 23 on your ACTS AT A
GLANCE chart.

DAY SEVEN

Store in your heart: Exodus 22:28.
Read and discuss: Acts 22:1-15; 23:11; John 15:16; Ephesians 2:10; Psalm 139:16; and Revelation 1:18.

OPTIONAL QUESTIONS FOR DISCUSSION

∾ As you studied Acts 22–23 what spoke to you the most or
impressed you the most?

∾ Where do you think Paul's boldness and confidence came
from? How was it manifested? What assurances did Paul
have from God? Look up Daniel 11:32b. How would this
verse give you insight into Paul's boldness and be a stimulus
to you?

∾ In these two chapters, how do you see the hand of God
carrying out His will for Paul? What does this show you
about God? How do the passages you read today under
"Read and discuss" go with this? What do you learn from
these verses? How could they help you through some difficult or even threatening situations?

∾ What did you learn from the way Paul conducted himself
before the various groups of people or individuals mentioned in these two chapters?

∾ What do you think Acts 23:5, which quotes Exodus 22:28,
means with respect to our leaders? Does this mean their sin
cannot be exposed, or does it refer to how we talk to them
or about them? Think about John the Baptist and Herod
(Luke 3:18-20) and then Paul and Ananias. What ought to
be our caution?

THOUGHT FOR THE WEEK

I don't know what kind of trials you are enduring at the moment, my friend. I know that whatever they are, they must be hard, and I know you want to handle them properly so that the Word of God and the character of God will not be soiled or diminished in any way with respect to others.

It's hard to look like the loser, to have others come against you. I understand, and when that happens, I run to the Word and find great relief, hope, and encouragement in the lives of our Savior and the apostle Paul. They weren't loved or even politely applauded by everyone. They endured all sorts of insults, accusations, and persecutions. Yet both endured until the end. They knew they were appointed by God . . . accounted as sheep for the slaughter, but they also knew they were more than conquerors.

You can know the same, Beloved. So live accordingly.

Unleashed for Obedience

DAY ONE

In these first several days of this week we will simply get an overview of Acts 24–26. Then we'll come back and look at each chapter in greater detail. Therefore, today read Acts 23:31–24:23. Note the city where Paul is and remember why he is there and how he got there. As you read this, remember what Paul was told in Acts 9:15 when he was saved! Note how God fulfills His Word.

DAY TWO

Read Acts 24:24–25:12. Mark the word *Caesar*. Caesar was the title given to the head of the Roman Empire. Look at the time chart on page 94 and note who the Caesar was and who was king over the Jews at the time of Paul's third missionary journey.

DAY THREE

Read Acts 25:13–26:32. Continue to mark any reference to Caesar.

DAY FOUR

Now, let's go back and dig a little deeper into these awesome chapters. They occur in that beautiful seaport of

THE HISTORY OF ISRAEL—THE GREEK AND ROMAN PERIODS

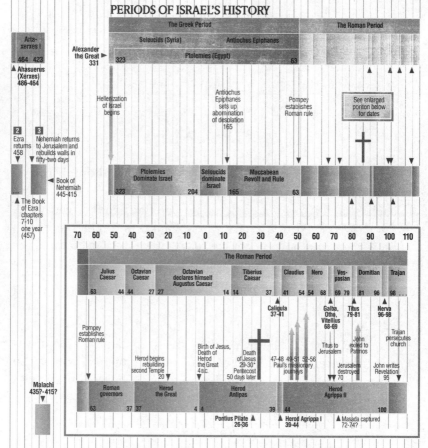

470 450 430 410 390 370 350 330 310 290 270 250 230 210 190 170 150 130 110 90 70 50 30 10 10 30 50 70 90 110

PERIODS OF ISRAEL'S HISTORY

The Greek Period · The Roman Period

Seleucids (Syria) · Antiochus Epiphanes

Alexander the Great ▶ 331 · 323 · Ptolemies (Egypt) · 63

Arta-xerxes I 464 423

▲ Ahasuerus (Xerxes) 486-464

Hellenization of Israel begins

Antiochus Epiphanes sets up abomination of desolation 165

Pompey establishes Roman rule

See enlarged portion below for dates

2 Ezra returns 458 ▼

3 Nehemiah returns to Jerusalem and rebuilds walls in fifty-two days

◀ Book of Nehemiah 445-415

... ▲ The Book of Ezra chapters 7-10 one year (457)

Ptolemies Dominate Israel 323 · 204

Seleucids dominate Israel 165

Maccabean Revolt and Rule 63

70 60 50 40 30 20 10 0 10 20 30 40 50 60 70 80 90 100 110

The Roman Period

Julius Caesar 63 44

Octavian Caesar 44 27

Octavian declares himself Augustus Caesar 27 14

Tiberius Caesar 14 37

Claudius 41 54

Nero 54 68

Vespasian 69 79

Domitian 81 96

Trajan 98 ...

Caligula 37-41

Galba, Otho, Vitellius 68-69

Titus 79-81

Nerva 96-98

Pompey establishes Roman rule

Herod begins rebuilding second Temple 20

Birth of Jesus, Death of Herod the Great 4 B.C.

Death of Jesus 29-30* Pentecost 50 days later

47-48 49-51 52-56 Paul's missionary journeys

Titus to Jerusalem

John exiled to Patmos

Jerusalem destroyed 70

John writes Revelation 95

Trajan persecutes church

Malachi 435?-415? ▼

Roman governors 63 37

Herod the Great 37 4

Herod Antipas 4 39

Herod Agrippa II 44 100

Pontius Pilate ▲ 26-36

▲ Herod Agrippa I 39-44

▲ Masada captured 72-74?

470 450 430 410 390 370 350 330 310 290 270 250 230 210 190 170 150 130 110 90 70 50 30 10 10 30 50 70 90 110

*Some scholars say 33 A.D.   IISB-47

Caesarea, where the Romans would often retreat to get away from Jerusalem.

Read Acts 24 and mark key words. Also mark expressions of time. Record in your notebook how long Paul was imprisoned in Caesarea.

As you read, also record everything you learn about Felix. It's quite interesting.

DAY FIVE

Now read Acts 25. Mark key words, locations, references to time. Note who comes on the scene in this chapter and what happens as a result.

DAY SIX

Acts 26 is Paul's defense before King Agrippa. Read it carefully and mark key words. If you learn anything new from this account of Paul's testimony, record it in your notebook. It's interesting to note what portion of his testimony Paul gives on these different occasions and the way he shares with those listening. Watch carefully how he handles the king. Does the king hear the gospel? Remember what the content of the gospel is.

Record your insights in your notebook. Also record the themes of chapters 24, 25, and 26 on the ACTS AT A GLANCE chart.

DAY SEVEN

♥ Store in your heart: Acts 26:18,19.
Read and discuss: Acts 9:15; Acts 26.

OPTIONAL QUESTIONS FOR DISCUSSION

∾ In Acts 1, why were the disciples told to wait in Jerusalem for the promise of the Father?

   a. What would happen when they were baptized with the Holy Spirit?

   b. What would they do for the Lord?

   c. What do you see happening in Acts 24–26?

∾ When you think of God's Word to Paul in Acts 9:15, do you think that Paul ever realized how this would be fulfilled? How did he handle himself? Discuss the way Paul dealt with all these officials and what you can learn from his example since you too are called to be a witness for the Lord Jesus Christ.

∾ What does Acts 26:18 tell you about what happens when those who are lost repent and believe on the Lord Jesus Christ? This Scripture is a wonderful verse to pray back to the Lord for those whom you know who are lost.

∾ List all the points that Paul deals with or presents to King Agrippa when he proclaims the gospel to him.

ᵒ⤳ According to Acts 26:22,23, what were the confines of Paul's message to King Agrippa? What should be the confines of our message? Is it enough? Is it adequate?

ᵒ⤳ What spoke to you the most as you studied Acts 24, 25, and 26?

THOUGHT FOR THE WEEK

Consequently, King Agrippa, I did not prove disobedient to the heavenly vision, but kept declaring...
(Acts 26:19,20).

As surely as the apostle Paul was called to proclaim the gospel, so are you, my friend, if you are a child of God. The same Spirit that worked in Paul is at work in you, both to will and to do of His good pleasure (Philippians 2:13). The calling is for a lifetime. The place is wherever He leads you—from your own "Jerusalem" to the world. The power is the Spirit, given to every child of God the moment he or she repents and believes.

Yet the responsibility is yours. You must be obedient. You must be willing to open your mouth, not fearing the face or position of any man or woman but only the disappointment or displeasure of your heavenly Father.

The results are God's. You cannot convert anyone, nor can you persuade someone to believe. That is between the hearer and God. So, keep on declaring the message without compromise. Watch what God does and where He takes you, whether it is before common men or before rulers and authorities. They all need the same message from a faithful messenger—the message that Jesus Christ died for our sins according to the Scriptures, that He was buried, but that He rose again, just as the Scriptures also said. Also, He was seen by many.

His Witness— by His Spirit!

Day One

Read Acts 27:1-17. As you read, examine the text in the light of the 5 W's and an H. Note the main characters, what is happening, when, where they go, what they do, and why. Underline every reference to location as you have done previously. Trace the ship's course on the map below.

Day Two

Read Acts 27:18-44. Once again ask and seek the answers to the 5 W's and an H. Mark all references to time. Trace the course of the ship on the map as you did yesterday.

DAY THREE

Read Acts 28:1-10. Once again examine the text as you have done the past two days. Watch for references to time and mark them. Mark any key words on your bookmark.

DAY FOUR

Read Acts 28:11-23. Mark key words, geographical locations, and references to time. You might want to mark every reference to the Jews (along with any synonyms or personal pronouns). Remember I mark these references with a blue star of David.

DAY FIVE

Look at the chart, SEQUENCE OF EVENTS IN PAUL'S LIFE AFTER HIS CONVERSION (page 55). Note the following so you can see the sequence of events. Next to each event fill in the year(s) when it occurred.

  a. In A.D. _____ Paul wrote the book of Romans.
  b. In A.D. _____ Paul went to Jerusalem where he was arrested and taken to Caesarea.
  c. In A.D. _____ Paul was sent from Caesarea to Rome.
  d. In A.D. _____ Paul arrived in Rome where he was imprisoned.

When Paul wrote his epistle to the Romans, what were *his* plans?

Read Romans 1:9-17 and Romans 15:20-33. Did Paul arrive in Rome as *he* planned? Was Paul delivered from those who were disobedient in Judea? To what degree or extent?

DAY SIX

Read Acts 28:23-31. Mark any key words on your list, along with every reference to the Jews. Also mark any reference to time, then look at the chart, SEQUENCE OF EVENTS IN PAUL'S LIFE AFTER HIS CONVERSION (page 55). Note what he accomplished during this Roman imprisonment in addition to what you are told in Acts 28:30-31.

Record the themes of Acts 27 and 28 on the ACTS AT A GLANCE chart.

DAY SEVEN

Store in your heart: Acts 28:27.

Read and discuss: Acts 28:20-31; Romans 1:16; Romans 9:30–10:4 (The word *end* in Romans 10:4 can be translated *goal.*)

OPTIONAL QUESTIONS FOR DISCUSSION

- Whenever Paul went into a new city to proclaim the gospel, where did he go first? Why do you think he did this?
- Who were the first to be called together after Paul arrived in Rome?
  a. What did you learn from the passage in Romans about Paul's concern for the salvation of the Jews?
  b. How great was that concern? How do you know?
  c. Do you think we are to be concerned about the Jews today?
  d. What is our responsibility to them with respect to the gospel?
- Do you think God has rejected the Jews? Read Romans 11:1-29.

a. Has God rejected the Jews because they as a nation have not repented and believed on the Lord Jesus Christ?

b. What do you learn about Jews who are being saved now? What are they called in verse 5?

c. If you take this passage literally (respecting the use of figures of speech such as similes and metaphors), is God finished with the Jews?

d. What does God's Word tell us will happen to the Jews? When will this happen?

∾ Discuss how Paul planned to go to Rome and how he ended up going there.

a. Do you think God placed Rome on Paul's heart?

b. Did God allow Paul to accomplish his heart's desire for going to Rome?

c. What do you learn from all this?

∾ Did Paul's circumstances diminish his zeal for the gospel or his commitment to it? What about you?

∾ What has been the most significant personal lesson you have gleaned from this study of Acts?

∾ What have you learned about the Holy Spirit from this study?

∾ What have you learned about proclaiming the gospel?

THOUGHT FOR THE WEEK

God says, "My ways are not your ways. . . ." Paul was a man who stepped out in faith, determined not to be disobedient to God's calling upon his life. He was a man who was determined that the grace of God would not be poured out on him for nothing—he would labor more than them all! Yet Paul acknowledged that it was not him, but the grace of God in him.

And so Paul stepped out in faith, and God led him all the way, step by step. Whether it was in accord with Paul's thoughts or plans did not matter. Paul knew and trusted his God because he knew that God's way was and is perfect. Thus, Paul seized the moment, whatever it was, whenever and wherever it came. By the power of the Spirit, Paul would be God's witness whether free or in chains!

And you and I are to do the same. The book of Acts ends with Acts 28:31, and yet it continues with us, you and me, "preaching the kingdom of God, and teaching concerning the Lord Jesus Christ with all openness, unhindered"—unhindered by anyone but ourselves.

Theme of Acts:

SEGMENT DIVISIONS

			CHAPTER THEMES	Author:
			1	
			2	Date:
			3	
			4	Purpose:
			5	
			6	
			7	Key Words:
			8	
			9	
			10	
			11	
			12	
			13	
			14	
			15	
			16	
			17	
			18	
			19	
			20	
			21	
			22	
			23	
			24	
			25	
			26	
			27	
			28	

THE INTERNATIONAL INDUCTIVE STUDY BIBLE IS

Changing the Way People Study God's Word

*I*T IS A REVOLUTIONARY IDEA whose time has come....a study Bible that actually teaches you *how* to study the Bible. As you follow simple, easy-to-understand instructions, you will discover God's truth on your own. In *The International Inductive Study Bible*, you will find maps right in the text where you need them, timeline charts showing biblical events in historical order, wide margins in which to write your notes, the accurate and reliable New American Standard Bible text, and dozens of other helpful features. This proven study method will lead you to experience God's Word in a way so personal, so memorable, that every insight you gain will be yours for life.

HARVEST HOUSE PUBLISHERS

1075 Arrowsmith, Eugene OR 97402

At bookstores everywhere!

YES! I am interested in information that will direct me to an Inductive Bible-study group in my area *or* that will help me or our church become involved in inductive Bible study.

Please have Precept Ministries contact me with details that will help me begin my inductive study right away!

NAME: _____

ADDRESS: _____

CITY: _____ STATE: _____ ZIP: _____

TELEPHONE NUMBER: (____) _____

Precept Ministries exists for the sole purpose of establishing God's people in His Word. The ministry serves hundreds of thousands of people across North America and around the globe by offering multiple and varied opportunities for training and inductive Bible study.

YOUR STAMP WILL HELP THE MINISTRY SAVE MONEY

BUSINESS REPLY MAIL
First Class Mail Permit No. 48 Chattanooga TN

POSTAGE WILL BE PAID BY ADDRESSEE

Precept Ministries
P.O. Box 182218
Chattanooga TN 37422-9901